# Alternative Energy

## BEYOND FOSSIL FUELS

by Dana Meachen Rau

Content Adviser: Teresa Kittridge, Executive Director,
Renewable Energy Marketplace—
Alliance for Talent Development

Science Adviser: Terrence E. Young Jr., M.Ed., M.L.S.,
Jefferson Parish (Louisiana) Public School System

Reading Adviser: Alexa L. Sandmann, Ed.D., Professor of Literacy,
College and Graduate School of Education, Health, and Human Services,
Kent State University

Compass Point Books
151 Good Counsel Drive
P.O. Box 669
Mankato, MN 56002-0669

This book was manufactured with paper containing
at least 10 percent post-consumer waste.

Photographs © Alamy Images: Adrian Sherratt 58, Images&Stories 30-31; Art Life Images: age
fotostock/Mark Turner 39, Stellar Stock/Michael Secam 34; BigStockPhoto.com: adifor 21; Capstone
Press: Karon Dubke 52(t); Corbis: Royalty-free/Leland Bobbé 60; Courtesy of www.boonepickens.
com 25; Getty Images Inc: Photographer's Choice/Mark Douet 53, Stone/Rita Maas 54; iStockphoto:
ason 13, fanelliphotography 38, Mlenny 15, photosbyjim 47, stevegeer 27(b), Terraxplorer 36, theasis
27(t), track5 5; Photodisc 44; Shutterstock: Al Mueller 24, Alexander Kalina 18, Baloncici 56, Brian A.
Jackson 22, bulankov 9, Chin-Cheng Liu 45(t), Daniel G. Mata 7, Fernando Delvalle 55, Floris Slooff
20, Graham Prentice 28, Jose Gill 46, Kiselev Andrey Valerevich 52(b), Konstantin Mironov 7(b), Lisa
F. Young 45(b), maxstockphoto 4, 12, 19, 26, 33, 40, 49, Meli78 17(t), Monkey Business Images 51,
Otmar Smit 14, Ronald van der Beek 42-43, Vibrant Image Studio 41, Zacarias Pereira da Mata 10.

Editor: Jennifer VanVoorst
Designer: Heidi Thompson
Media Researcher: Wanda Winch
Art Director: LuAnn Ascheman-Adams
Creative Director: Joe Ewest
Editorial Director: Nick Healy
Managing Editor: Catherine Neitge

**Library of Congress Cataloging-in-Publication Data**
Rau, Dana Meachen, 1971–
  Alternative energy: beyond fossil fuels / by Dana Meachen Rau.
    p. cm. — (Green generation)
  Includes bibliographical references and index.
  ISBN 978-0-7565-4247-4 (library binding)
  ISBN 978-0-7565-4289-4 (paperback)
  1. Renewable energy sources—Juvenile literature.
  2. Power resources—Juvenile literature. I. Title. II. Series.
  TJ808.2.R38 2010
  333.79'4—dc22                  2009008778

Visit Compass Point Books on the Internet at www.capstonepub.com

# Contents

> "It is time to make peace with the planet."
> —Al Gore, environmental activist, Nobel Prize winner, and former vice president of the United States

# Running on Empty

## introduction

You need energy to start your day. Your breakfast is the fuel your body needs to work. What would you do if you ran out of your favorite cereal? You could buy another box. But what if the store was all out, too? What if it wasn't getting any more deliveries? What would you do then? The answer seems simple. You'd have to find another food for breakfast.

The world faces a similar problem. Our fuel sources are running low and could run out in your lifetime, but you can help do something about it. Together we can find alternatives.

**Power sources:** Most everything in the world needs energy to work. Think about the energy you use each day: the lights you turn on, the bus or car you take to school, the computer you use for homework, the television you watch before bed. Even while you sleep, energy runs the furnace heating your house and the refrigerator keeping food from spoiling. It even runs the alarm clock that wakes you up in the morning. Now think about how many people live on Earth. With a population of more than 6 billion, the world uses a lot of energy.

Using a computer consumes energy, but laptops use less energy than desktop computers.

Think about all the energy that goes into making a piece of toast:

- A farmer plows the field, grows the grain, and harvests it using equipment that needs gasoline to run.
- A diesel truck brings the grain to a mill.
- Electric machines at the mill grind the grain into flour, and other machines bag the flour.
- A truck takes the flour to another factory.
- This factory uses machines to combine the flour with other ingredients and bake the bread.
- More machines bag the bread.
- A truck delivers the bread to stores.
- People drive to the store to buy bread.
- An electric toaster turns the bread into toast.

Whew! That's a lot of energy! And we didn't even mention all of the workers at the farm and factories who drove to work. Or the plastic company that makes the bags for the bread. Or the electricity needed to light a huge grocery store.

GO DEEP

People rely on energy for three main uses: transportation, electricity, and heating and cooling. We use fossil fuels to create this energy. These ancient sources formed from the remains of plants hundreds of millions of years ago. Sediment covered the dead plant matter and formed into rock. More layers of rock formed above, and the pressure of this rock turned the remains into coal, oil, and natural gas, our three main fossil fuels.

**Coal:** People mine for coal, a hard, black rock, throughout the world. Power plants use coal to generate electricity by grinding it into a powder that is burned. The burning powder heats water to create steam. The power of the steam turns turbines. The spinning motion of the turbines generates electricity. A network of wires, called a power grid, brings this electricity to houses and other buildings.

**Oil:** Companies drill for oil on land or in the ocean and store it in large barrels or underground tanks. People turn oil into many products, including plastics. Your ballpoint pen, your nylon backpack, and even your

Coal is often mined in open pits when the deposits are near the surface.

## Atoms That Pack a Punch

Nuclear power is energy created by splitting uranium atoms. It's already in wide use, and some people support using even more nuclear power as an energy alternative. Compared with other fossil fuels, uranium is not expensive to mine. And while uranium is not a renewable resource, Earth has a large supply.

Nuclear power doesn't emit harmful gases. However, the process of splitting atoms does create toxic waste, which must be securely contained and stored so that it doesn't contaminate the environment. Furthermore, accidents at nuclear power plants are dangerous and can even be deadly. Still, many believe nuclear power to be an energy source worthy of more widespread use.

fleece jacket are all made from oil. Some homes burn oil for heat, and some power plants burn oil, too. In the United States, however, oil's main use is for transportation. Oil is made into gasoline for cars, diesel fuel for trucks, and jet fuel for airplanes.

**Natural gas:** Companies drill for natural gas the way they do for oil. Natural gas is highly flammable. Gas stoves cook food with a low flame. Your home's heating system and water heater may use natural gas. Natural gas is also used in power plants to create electricity.

**The problems:** Fossil fuels have been a useful source of energy, but we need to rethink how much we depend on them. We need to consider three main facts. First, fossil fuel supplies are low. We use so much energy that

some day we'll use up all of Earth's fossil fuels. At the rate we now use fossil fuels, scientists estimate that the world's reserves will last 40 to 70 more years. What will happen after all of the oil, coal, and natural gas have run out? How will we travel from place to place? How will we light our homes? How will we communicate with each other?

The second fact is that fossil fuels cost a lot of money. Countries buy fossil fuels from each other. Because the supply is low, they can raise their prices. If countries go to war or have a disagreement, they may not want to buy fuel from each other. No one will get what they need.

Finally, burning fossil fuels harms Earth. Coal, oil, and natural gas create a lot of air pollution. The burning of fossil fuels releases harmful emissions that cause asthma and other health problems. This pollution also leads to acid rain and snow. Many scientists and citizens are concerned about the amount of carbon dioxide released by burning fossil fuels. Carbon dioxide belongs to a group of gases known as greenhouse gases. As these gases collect in the atmosphere, they act like the glass walls of a greenhouse, trapping warm air close to Earth's surface. This warming is natural, and long ago it made the planet's environment mild enough to support life. However, when human activities pump larger-than-normal amounts of carbon dioxide into the atmo-

Gases and pollutants released by burning fossil fuels cause global warming, as well as various health problems.

sphere, more heat is trapped, and temperatures can grow unnaturally high. As a result, there can be major effects on weather that may be devastating to the environment and all the people on Earth.

**The solutions:** What can we do about our energy problems? Instead of relying on fossil fuels, we need to examine our "green" alternatives. Green energy is renewable—it is constantly being replaced and won't run out. Natural forces such as wind, water, and sunlight are green energy sources.

It's not easy to switch over to green energy, however. We rely on fossil fuels every day. People would need to spend huge amounts of money to change from one kind of fuel to another.

We need to take action, but first we need to understand our energy alternatives. Then we can make the best energy choices to preserve our planet.

## By the Numbers

### Energy Use in the United States Today

| | |
|---|---|
| oil | 40% |
| natural gas | 24% |
| coal | 23% |
| nuclear | 8% |
| renewable energy | 7% |
| electricity imports | 0.1% |

| | |
|---|---|
| ethanol & biomass | 3.6% |
| hydroelectric | 2.4% |
| geothermal | 0.35% |
| wind | 0.3% |
| solar | 0.08% |

> "If everybody used half as much electricity, it would change the world."
> —Bill Nye, The Science Guy, television host

# Solar Energy
## LIVING OFF THE GRID

chapter 1

Put on sunglasses, rub in sunscreen, and hit the beach. It's time to soak up some rays! The sun can give you a great tan or make you sweat playing Frisbee. The sun's light and heat can also help us solve our energy problems.

You have probably noticed wires running from your home to poles on the street. These wires connect you to the power grid of your community. Homes that use solar power don't need as much energy from the grid. There are two types of solar power: solar cell energy and solar thermal energy.

## How solar cells work:

Years ago scientists developed solar cells, also called photovoltaic cells or PV cells, which can turn the sun's light directly into electricity. These small, flat devices made of silicon come in a variety of sizes. You may have seen PV cells in a calculator. Some billboards and streetlights use PV cells to operate. Most cells are about 4 inches by 4 inches (10 centimeters by 10 centimeters) and grouped together in panels on the roofs of buildings. The solar panels absorb the sun's light and transform it into electric current. The electricity can then run lights, machines, and appliances in the buildings. The more PV cells, the more electricity the panels can create.

Photovoltaic cells are made of silicon, the primary element in sand.

The cells generate electrical power when the sun is shining. But what happens at night or when the sun is covered by clouds? Batteries store the electricity. Because solar panels absorb light, not heat, they still create electricity during a cold winter. As long as the sun is shining, PV cells are at work.

Your family can install solar panels on your home, even though you are connected to the power grid. At times, the panels may even generate more power than your home needs. The power company then buys any extra power you create and puts it back into the grid for someone else to use. So by using solar panels, you can help your whole community rely more on a green energy source.

In the Northern Hemisphere, solar panels must face south and be angled to receive maximum sunlight.

## How solar thermal energy works:

Solar thermal energy uses heat instead of light. People can place thermal panels on their roofs to absorb the sun's heat. Tubing filled with water runs under the panels. The sun warms the water. This water can then be used to make a cup of cocoa, fill a swimming pool, or run through a home's heating system.

Thermal energy can also create electricity. In a solar power plant, the sun heats a liquid until it boils. Then the steam created from this boiling liquid runs a turbine to generate electricity. In order for the liquids to boil, these power plants use mirrors to focus the sun's heat and increase its strength. Some mirrors

Mirrors increase the intensity of the sun's heat, creating more power.

are curved and shaped like a saucer. Others are shaped like a trough or placed in a line. Some new solar energy plants have a power tower. Thousands of mirrors surround the tower and focus the sun's heat to the top.

## A great solution:

Solar energy sounds like a great solution to the energy problem. Energy from the sun is free and clean. The sun isn't in danger of running out. Converting the sun's light and heat into usable energy doesn't create any air or water pollution.

Solar energy also gives us options, with more than one way to create electricity. It can even work within the power grid system that already exists. Power plants could switch from burning

## Tower of Power

In Australia plans are under way to build a tower in an area where the sun shines 300 or more days a year. Rising almost 3,300 feet (1,000 meters), it will be nearly twice as tall as the tallest building in the world. The tower will be surrounded by a vast panel of glass. The sun will heat the air under the glass. Since hot air rises, the air will rush toward the tower with enough speed to turn turbines and create electricity. The electricity will feed into a nearby power station and supply about 200,000 homes.

Solar panels are often placed in the desert because of the vast amount of open space.

coal or other fossil fuels to using the steam from solar-heated water instead.

## Challenges of solar energy: The sun has to shine for cells to create electricity or to warm thermal panels. Even when the sun is out, the amount of sunlight isn't the same in all areas.

Large open spaces, such as deserts, are ideal places for solar plants. However, these plants could disrupt the wildlife of the desert since they need to cover such a large area.

Cost is a problem, too. If your parents decide to put solar panels on your house, they can decrease the amount of electricity they need to buy from the power company. However, it costs a lot of money to buy and install solar panels in the first place. Creating solar cells is also expensive. Furthermore, the manufacture of silicon for PV cells creates some waste products that go back into the environment.

Researchers are looking for ways to solve these problems. They're trying to find other materials for making cells. They're also experimenting with thinner cells so they don't need to use as much silicon. They're considering ways to make solar panels less expensive as well.

## A Race to Alternative Energy

Eager fans at the Dell-Winston School Solar Car Challenge hope for a sunny day. The cars they are waiting to watch don't use gasoline. They use the sun to run. The Dell-Winston School Solar Car Challenge is an annual competition of high school teams. They race their solar cars at the Texas Motor Speedway or on cross-country trips of more than 2,000 miles (3,200 kilometers). The cars collect energy with PV cells. The student designers have to create cars that will absorb the maximum amount of energy from the sun.

> *"First, there is the power of the wind, constantly exerted over the globe. ... Here is an almost incalculable power at our disposal, yet how trifling the use we make of it! It only serves to turn a few mills, blow a few vessels across the ocean, and a few trivial ends besides. What a poor compliment do we pay to our indefatigable and energetic servant!"*
> —Henry David Thoreau, 19th century author and environmentalist

# Wind Energy

## OLD MACDONALD HAD A TURBINE

chapter 2

You know that farms produce fruit, grain, and even milk. But do you know that there are wind farms, too? Instead of rows of crops, you'll find rows of turbines on a wind farm.

Wind is moving air. The motion is caused by changes in air temperature. Warm air is light, and cold air is heavy. When the land heats up during the day, it warms the air above it. This warm air rises higher in the sky, while cold air moves down to fill the space left by the warm air. This movement of air creates wind.

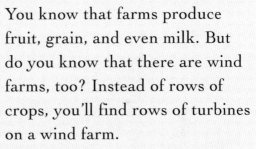

Wind can be powerful, as with a destructive hurricane, but its power can also be used for good. Sailors use the wind to keep their sailboats moving. Throughout history people have used windmills to harness the wind's energy for grinding grain or pumping well water. Today people use wind turbines to generate electricity.

## How wind power works:

A wind turbine has what looks like an airplane propeller mounted very high on a tower. The blades of the turbine catch the wind and spin. The blades spin a shaft that is connected to an electrical generator. Wires connect the generator to the power grid to bring electricity to buildings in the area.

To increase the amount of

The Netherlands is famous for its old windmills, which were used to grind grain and pump water.

As wind spins the blades of a wind turbine, the motion is transferred to a generator, which creates electricity.

power, turbines are often grouped in wind farms. Most wind farms aren't owned by electric power companies. They're owned by "wind farmers" who sell the electricity to power companies.

Wind turbines work best where wind blows strongest. Wind is usually stronger the higher you go. That's why turbines are often mounted on tall towers or placed on the tops of hills. Some towers stand between 100 and 250 feet (30 and 76 m) high. Shorelines and wide-open prairies are also good places for towers. Turbines don't work well in locations with too many mountains, forests, or buildings, which block the wind's flow. Some people place small turbines on their roofs and position them in a way to catch the most wind.

**A great solution:** The center of the United States is the windiest part of the country and one of the windiest areas of the world. A lot of states already have wind energy programs. People are also developing plans for offshore wind farms in places such as Cape Cod, Massachusetts, where wind is also strong. In the past 10 years, an increasing number of people have turned to wind power. It's one of the fastest growing types of alternative energy.

Wind is clean and free. It doesn't create air or water pollution. Wind won't run out either. It is created as long as the sun keeps on warming the land.

More and more farmers are erecting turbines on their land to farm wind as well as crops.

## The Top 10 Wind-Power Producing States

1. Texas (7,118 megawatts* generating capacity)
2. Iowa (2,791 MW)
3. California (2,517 MW)
4. Minnesota (1,752 MW)
5. Washington (1,447 MW)
6. Colorado (1,068 MW)
7. Oregon (1,067 MW)
8. Illinois (915 MW)
9. New York (832 MW)
10. Kansas (815 MW)

*A megawatt (MW) is equal to 1 million watts. A watt is a measure of electrical power. For example, a 100-watt bulb uses 100 watts of electricity.

## Challenges of wind energy:

Even in the windiest places, wind doesn't always blow. To run a turbine, wind needs to blow at more than 7.5 miles per hour (12 kph). If the wind is not strong enough, the turbines won't spin. No spinning means no electricity. Furthermore, it's not as easy to store wind-generated electricity as it is other types. So power plants that use wind-generated electricity often need back up energy sources, such as fossil fuels.

Wind farms require large

areas of land, which can affect both the landscape and the animals in an area.

Turbines are also a danger to birds that fly into the propellers, although the number of birds that die from turbines is tiny compared with those that die from flying into windows.

Starting a wind farm costs a lot of money, too. A large utility-scale turbine can cost more than $1 million. As with other forms of alternative energy, people continue to look for ways to keep costs down.

# By the Numbers

## The 10 States With the Most Wind Energy Potential

1. North Dakota
2. Texas
3. Kansas
4. South Dakota
5. Montana
6. Nebraska
7. Wyoming
8. Oklahoma
9. Minnesota
10. Iowa

## Oil Man to Green Man

T. Boone Pickens is a Texas billion-aire whose family grew rich in the oil business. Still, Pickens is not happy that the United States depends so much on other countries to buy the fuels it needs. He wants to reduce the amount of fuel the country imports by focusing on wind energy.

Pickens would like Americans to replace the amount of natural gas they now use for electricity—about 22 percent—with wind energy. He thinks it can be done in the next 10 years if people really make the effort. To help his "Pickens Plan" get started, he's investing $10 billion to build a wind farm in Texas. It would be the largest in the world.

> " *Everything in nature contains all the power of nature. Everything is made of one hidden stuff.*"
> –Ralph Waldo Emerson, 19th century author

# Geothermal Energy

## EARTH WORKING FOR US

chapter 3

Old Faithful, Yellowstone National Park's most famous geyser, erupts with thousands of gallons of water and steam every hour to hour and a half. This popular Wyoming tourist spot is home to more than 60 percent of the world's geysers. In just one square mile (2.6 square kilometers), you can see more than 150 of them.

Some people think of Earth as a solid ball of rock, but it has many layers. At the center, Earth has a solid core. Around this core is an area of hot, liquid rock called magma. Above the magma is a layer of solid rock and magma called the mantle. The temperature of the mantle can be very high — from 2,520 to 5,400 degrees Fahrenheit (1,382 to 2,982 degrees Celsius), depending on how deep you go. The surface of Earth, the crust, sits on the mantle.

Water sometimes collects in the rocks underground and heats up. If there is a vent leading from this deep rock to the surface, superheated water shoots upward. Earth's crust is thicker in some areas than others. In Yellowstone, the hot mantle is only a few miles below the surface. That's why the park has so many geysers.

So why not let Earth work

Yellowstone's North Geyser Basin is an area with a lot of of geothermal energy.

for us? We can use the planet's intense heat, called geothermal energy, to create electrical power. Geothermal means "earth heat."

## How geothermal energy works: Most

power plants today run from the power of steam created by burning fossil fuels. Instead we could use steam created by Earth to turn the turbines to generate electricity.

To harness geothermal energy, a power company drills deep down to reach a natural reservoir of water. The water's temperature is 300 to 700 F (149 to 371 C). The hot water is brought to the surface, where its steam is used to turn the electricity-generating turbines. The steam then condenses back into water and returns to the underground reservoir

Iceland has many geothermal power plants.

through another well. Then it can be heated again by Earth. No water is wasted.

Another way to use geothermal energy is by running water pipes underground. Earth's natural underground heat warms the water in the pipes. This water can be collected in wells and then pumped to houses and other buildings.

Many countries already use geothermal power in this way, including the United States and Iceland. Iceland heats about 90 percent of its homes with

## By the Numbers

## Top 10 Countries With the Most Installed Generating Capacity of Geothermal Energy

1. United States (2,544 megawatt equivalents)
2. Philippines (1,931 MWe)
3. Mexico (953 MWe)
4. Indonesia (797 MWe)
5. Italy (790 MWe)
6. Japan (535 MWe)
7. New Zealand (435 MWe)
8. Iceland (322 MWe)
9. Costa Rica (163 MWe)
10. El Salvador (151 MWe)

geothermal energy. Because Iceland is in a very active volcanic area, the magma under the island nation is close to the surface. So the temperature underground is perfect for heating water.

**A great solution:** Inside Earth, the temperature is always high—every day, all day. Unlike with the sun and wind, the amount of heat never varies. So geothermal energy seems like a great solution to our energy problems. No fuels need to be burned to create steam, so the air stays clean. Geothermal plants can operate all the

Iceland's Svartsengi power plant is connected to the Blue Lagoon geothermal spa.

time, and they don't depend on the weather. Earth does all the work for us!

## Challenges of geothermal energy:

This solution makes sense to nations that have geothermal energy close to the surface. Not all places in the world have easy access to these hot reservoirs of water, though. Furthermore, the superheated reservoirs do eventually dry up.

Researchers in the United

States, France, Australia, and other countries have proposed injecting water to create artificial underground reservoirs. Machines would drill deep to reach hot rock, and cold water would be pumped down to create a reservoir. Earth would heat the water, and then we could bring it back to the surface to generate electricity.

But drilling through some types of rock, such as granite, is not easy. Costs could be high. Researchers estimate it would cost $1 billion to test this new technology. A billion dollars may seem like a lot of money, but it costs a lot to create a coal-burning plant, too. Geothermal energy is certainly a power source worth our attention.

# By the Numbers

## The Fabulous Four

The United States generates more geothermal electricity than any other country. But the amount of electricity produced this way is less than one-half of one percent of all electricity produced in the United States. Currently only four states have geothermal power plants:

- **California** has 33 plants that produce almost 90 percent of the nation's geothermal electricity.
- **Nevada** has 14 geothermal power plants.
- **Hawaii** and **Utah** each has one plant.

"When one tugs at a single thing in nature, he finds it attached to the rest of the world."
—John Muir, environmentalist and founder of the Sierra Club in 1892

# Hydro Energy

## GOING WITH THE FLOW

### chapter 4

Water in nature is constantly moving. Waves crash against beaches, and tides pull water from shores. Rapids rush over rocks in a river. Waterfalls cascade over cliffs. Water is another renewable resource on our planet. In fact it's the most abundant. You don't have to look far to find water—it covers more than 75 percent of Earth! We can harness some of its power to create electricity. "Hydro" means water. Hydroelectric power plants are already in use. Water runs nearly 10 percent of power plants in the United States. In fact water is the leading renewable energy source used to generate electric power.

## How hydropower works: Rivers are a natural source of flowing water. Hydroelectric power plants use this energy. Plants are built across rivers, and the water flows through turbines. The turbines spin and create electricity.

Sometimes power companies build dams across rivers. A dam stops the river's flow. The area of still water behind the dam becomes a reservoir. By using a dam, the flow of water can be better controlled. Pipes or tunnels channel the water to turbines. Then the water exits out the other side of the dam.

Washington's Grand Coulee Dam is the largest hydroelectric facility in the United States.

## Water Power Is Nothing New

Throughout history people have harnessed the power of water to create energy. From the time of the ancient Romans through the late 1800s, water mills have been used to grind grain and run machines. A water mill is a large wooden wheel mounted on the side of a building next to a river. Sometimes the water is channeled over the top of the wheel. The water falls onto blades on the wheel to make it spin. Other times the wheel is placed right into the river. The flowing water of the river pushes the blades on the wheel to make it turn. The wheel is connected to the machines inside the building. The spinning motion of the wheel moves the parts of the machines.

Besides flowing rivers, researchers also experiment with other sources of hydropower. The constant motion of ocean waves is a powerful force. An oscillating water column was designed in Japan to harness the rising and falling of waves. Shaped like a round chimney, the column lets in ocean waves at the bottom. The waves rise in the chamber. Each time a wave pushes up, the rising wave forces air out of the chamber. This air pushes a turbine that generates electricity.

Tides can also turn turbines. A tidal barrage is a dam that spreads across an inlet, a place where the ocean comes into the land. As the tide comes in, water flows through turbines, generating electricity. Then the water collects in a reservoir behind the barrage. As the tide pulls the water out, the water passes through the turbines

The flow of water spins large turbines in a dam to generate electricity.

again. So a tidal barrage can generate electricity during both high and low tides.

Researchers are also developing tidal turbines that would work a lot like wind turbines. Mounted underwater, the turbines would spin as strong tides pass by them.

**A great solution:** Water will never run out. It evaporates into the air and then falls as rain or snow. This water cycle never ends, so we don't have to worry about using up all the water on Earth.

Hydropower has already been tested, and it works. Unlike burning fuels, hydropower doesn't create air pollution. Nothing is cleaner than a flowing river!

**The challenges of hydropower:** Water may cover most of Earth, but that doesn't mean all communities

# By the Numbers

## The 10 States That Create the Most Hydro Electricity

1. Washington
2. Oregon
3. California
4. New York
5. Idaho
6. Montana
7. Arizona
8. Tennessee
9. Alabama
10. Arkansas

have access to a good water source for hydropower. Companies build hydro-electric power plants in mountainous areas where there are a lot of rivers with powerful flows. A hydro-electric plant wouldn't make sense in a dry, flat area.

Making hydropower also affects nearby wildlife and the environment. Dams block the travel paths of some fish. Flooding the land behind a dam destroys farmland and forests. Animals and people are forced to leave the area. In the ocean, tidal barrages affect the natural cycle of tidal creatures, block the paths of larger sea animals, and may affect boaters and swimmers in the area.

Tide and wave technology would only work in

Dams are often built in mountainous areas, where water in rivers runs quickly downstream.

Fish ladders help spawning fish get back upstream, minimizing the environmental impact of dams.

shoreline communities. Furthermore, tidal barrages need inlets with a range of more than 100 feet (30 m) between high and low tide. Few places in the world meet that condition. France and Canada use commercial tidal barrages, but there are only a few other countries, such as England and Russia, where it would even be possible.

Some countries are devel-oping more uses for wave energy. Good sites have been considered in the United States, Europe, and New Zealand. Still, wave energy devices have only been proven to work on a small scale. People will have to consider whether the cost of larger, commercial devices is worth it.

"Let's be the generation that finally frees America from the tyranny of oil. We can harness homegrown alternative fuels like ethanol and spur the production of more fuel-efficient cars. ... Let's be the generation that makes future generations proud of what we did here."
     -Barack Obama, 44th president of the United States

# Biomass Energy

## MOVING TOWARD CHANGE

### chapter 5

Think of how much trash your family creates each week. Do you fill one garbage can? Do you fill two? Now think of how many people live in your neighborhood, your town, your state. All that trash adds up.

A lot of the trash people throw away can be reused. Many towns have recycling programs for glass, plastic, and metal. Even "natural trash" can be used for energy instead of sending it to the landfill.

Biomass refers to organic material that can be made into usable energy. Wood is biomass.

People have used wood since the beginning of history for heat and light. Today many people still heat their homes with a fireplace or wood stove. That's using biomass energy.

## Biomass and biogas:

Have you ever helped your parents clean up your yard or a park? You might have raked up lawn clippings, fallen leaves, and tree branches. You may have dumped them in the woods, or bagged them and put them on your curb for pickup. But this biomass could be used to generate electricity.

Just as fossil fuels are burned to boil water and create steam, we can burn biomass for the same reason. All yard waste, as well as paper waste from paper mills, leftover crops, and

When people burn wood, they are using biomass energy.

even sawdust from lumber mills, can be burned in power plants.

Power plants can also burn biogas, such as methane. When natural materials in landfills break down, they release a gas called methane. The manure from livestock on farms also releases methane. This gas harms Earth's atmosphere, but it

Cattle and other livestock release methane as part of their digestive processes.

can be burned like natural gas. Pipes can channel methane gas from landfills and farms to generators that create electricity.

**Biofuel:** Think about how excited you get before a vacation. Your family packs up the car and you're ready to go. Sometimes lots of families have the same idea. You end up stuck in traffic with hundreds of other cars.

Burning gasoline creates a lot of air pollution. That doesn't even count the pollution created by airplanes using jet fuel or trucks burning diesel. Sometimes in cities, air thick with smog is hard to even breathe. People believe we can make cleaner fuels with biomass energy. Fuel made from biomass is called biofuel.

The biofuel ethanol is made from corn grown specifically to be turned into fuel. The corn is ground down and then heated with enzymes to turn it into a sugar. It is processed further to become ethanol. People are also looking to other crops, such as grasses, sugarcane, trees, and potatoes, as sources of ethanol.

Another alternative fuel is biodiesel. Biodiesel is not as

Cars are one of the biggest emitters of carbon dioxide.

difficult to make as ethanol. Vegetable oils, such as corn oil, peanut oil, or sunflower oil, can become biodiesel.

Researchers are considering an oil produced by algae. Biodiesel can even be made from the oil left over from cooking french fries!

## A great solution:

Using biomass energy cuts down on waste. We can use natural sources that would normally be thrown away to create various kinds of biofuel.

Ethanol has already been accepted as a good replacement for gasoline. In fact, since the early 1990s, it's been blended with gasoline to lower the cost of fuel. New laws may require that gasoline include even more ethanol. Scientists are developing trees and grasses that grow quickly in many climates and

Ethanol-blended gasoline is becoming increasingly available at gas stations across the United States.

## Plug-in Hybrids

Instead of just finding replacements for gasoline, carmakers are redesigning their cars to be more efficient. Traditional cars have large gas-burning engines. Hybrid cars have smaller gas engines, as well as electrical engines that run by battery power.

Car designers are taking this idea a step further. Plug-in hybrids have extra-large batteries and run almost completely on electricity. A person charges his or her car by plugging it into an electrical outlet.

Ethanol plants—and farms that grow and process corn for ethanol—are common throughout the Midwest.

are designed to yield a high amount of ethanol.

## The challenges of biomass energy: Using

biofuel cuts down on the use of oil for gasoline. But huge areas of land are needed to grow the crops to process into biofuels. Where would farmers grow crops for food? Some people wonder whether we have enough farmland to grow both types of crops.

Any type of burning releases pollution into the air. Biomass or biogas burned for electrical energy does emit harmful carbon dioxide, but not as much as burning fossil fuels. The good news is that plants take carbon dioxide out of the air to help them grow. So if biomass is burned close to a farm with fields of new plants, the crops would take in the carbon dioxide emitted.

## Speak Out for Hydrogen

Do you have a concern? Speak out! Teenager Jaclyn D'Arcy did. She was concerned about the future of transportation energy, so she started Kids 4 Hydrogen, an organization in support of hydrogen fuel technology for cars. Its members believe in producing hydrogen in clean, renewable ways through solar energy. The hydrogen created could then be fed into a fuel cell, which would convert it into electricity.

Hydrogen energy is already being used on the space shuttle and in some cars and buses. It is also being used to heat houses and other buildings. Hydrogen fuel cells are a promising energy source worthy of further research.

> "One person can make a difference, and every person should try."
> –John F. Kennedy, 35th president of the United States

# Saving Energy Is a Solution, Too!

chapter 6

We may be running low on fossil fuels, but our energy future still looks bright. Earth has always provided what we need to live. We just need to examine the alternative sources of energy our planet has to offer.

We can use Earth's natural energy sources, such as sun, wind, heat, and water. We can reuse natural trash or grow crops to create energy. All of these options are environmentally friendly and use renewable energy. They all have good points. They all come with challenges, too. So what's the solution?

# The solution is YOU!

Right now adults make a lot of choices for you. Your parents, teachers, and government set the rules that affect how you live. They are making a lot of the decisions about the types of energy we'll use in our future. But some scientists think fossil fuels will run out in your lifetime, so you need to be part of the discussion.

Do you think about how much energy you use every day? A carbon footprint is how much carbon dioxide a person, organization, or location lets into the atmosphere. Many Internet sites have carbon footprint calculators to help you see how much carbon dioxide you create. The calculator asks you how much energy your home uses for electricity. It asks you how often you take

## Help From the Top

Government agencies set energy policies in the United States. Officials look at the choices and decide where to spend money. Sometimes the government offers tax benefits to get people to switch to alternative energy. For example, your family wouldn't have to pay as much in taxes if you had a hybrid car, bought energy-efficient appliances, used biofuels, or installed wind turbines or solar panels on your home.

trips in airplanes, and how often you use a car or bus. It considers your eating habits, your clothes, and what you do for fun. Then it calculates how all of your energy use affects the environment.

It will take a while for the world to switch to alternative energy. For now think of saving energy as a solution, too. Instead of creating a big carbon footprint, we can each take steps toward using less energy as we look for other energy sources.

## The first step: Save your energy: Take an "energy walk" around your house. You'll be amazed at all the energy you waste. Lightbulbs use a lot of

Reduce your home energy and water use by running only full loads in your dishwasher.

electricity. By switching to compact fluorescent bulbs, you can burn about 75 percent less electricity than with regular bulbs. Ask yourself whether you really need the light on. Could you read by a sunny window instead? Turning lights off during the day or when you leave a room saves a lot of energy.

Many appliances still use electricity even when they're turned off. Any appliance with a clock, such as a microwave or DVD player, is always using energy. A television is always in standby mode so it is ready when you press the remote. This

You use solar energy when you read by the light from a window.

Using compost helps enrich your garden naturally.

constant use of energy is called a phantom load. Cut down the phantom load by turning off or unplugging appliances that don't need to run when you're not using them. You could turn off the monitor when you shut your computer down, and don't leave the chargers for your phone or MP3 player plugged in all the time.

Also think about what you put in the trash can. Don't throw away natural trash, such as banana peels or apple cores. If you have a garden, toss them into a compost heap. They'll turn into rich soil to help new plants grow. Instead of tossing away a sheet of paper, use the back side, too. Recycle items at your town's recycling center. Use a glass bottle as a vase. Use

Take your lunch to school in reuseable
containers to cut down on trash.

an empty cup as a pencil holder. Look at how you pack your lunch. Do you use a separate plastic bag for each food item? Do you bring a juice box or bottle of water? Your lunch creates a lot of trash. Why not bring a reusable container and water bottle instead?

## The second step: Helping the community: You've taken care of the things within your control. Now take a look at your community. How can you help everyone conserve and think about alternative energy sources?

You could take public transportation, ride a bike,

plates that could be washed and used again. Washing uses energy — heating the water and running the dishwasher — but your school could install energy-efficient appliances and a solar thermal panel to heat the water.

or carpool to school or a game. All of these forms of transportation reduce the number of cars on the road. Fewer cars means less gasoline is used. Bikes are the most healthful option for the environment — and the rider, too!

Look at your school. Does the cafeteria use disposable trays, utensils, or plates? There would be less waste if no trays were used at all. Or the cafeteria could use trays, utensils, and

## Check It

### Small Steps You Can Take Today

- Take a short shower.
- Turn off the lights when you leave a room.
- Put on a sweater instead of turning up the heat.
- Recycle your soda can.
- Throw your apple core in the compost heap.
- Reuse a plastic bag.
- Ride your bike instead of taking the car.

Farmers markets are a great source of environmentally friendly food.

Are there farms in your area? Eating foods grown or produced near your home reduces energy use. That's because trucks don't need to drive across the country to deliver the foods to stores. They only have to drive from the field to the farm stand, or down the road to the local grocery store.

## The third step: Spreading the word about alternatives:

You can't solve all our energy problems on your own, but you can get energized about the solutions. Now that you know some of the alternatives, how will you share the news?

## How Can I Save the World (Without Becoming a Superhero)?

Why not start an environmental club with your friends? Change the World Kids is a group started by teens in Vermont who take on problems and start their own programs to help save the world. Their Save Energy for Free program helps people in their community. They urge people to use the sun and wind to dry clothes outside instead of using a lot of energy running a clothes dryer. A team from Change the World Kids even installs clotheslines. Then they ask people to keep a journal and record how much energy they save.

You can tell your friends about alternative energy. You can tell your parents. You can join clubs in school or community organizations that talk about green energy. Many states have alternative energy programs. You can help spread the word.

You can get the word out through flyers, a Web site, or a blog. You can wear an alternative energy T-shirt. You can encourage government representatives who propose laws and policies. So let your voice be heard. Together we can improve our

Environmental careers are growing in number; one could be in your future!

## Be Paid to Make a Difference

By the time you're looking for a job, there will be lots more in the renewable energy industry than there are today. Think of the skills you have and the subjects that interest you:

- If you like science, you could be a researcher, studying Earth, the sun, or the weather.

- If you like working with your hands, you could work in construction, building more energy-efficient homes.

- If you are creative, you could be a designer, developing plans for a new type of turbine or fuel-efficient car.

- If you like to talk to people, you could be in sales, persuading people to buy your environmentally friendly products.

- If you like the outdoors, you could be a farmer, growing specialized crops to be used for biofuel.

No matter what your skills are, there's a green job for you. You can be paid to make a difference!

GO DEEP

Remember to reduce, reuse, and recycle. Small changes will improve the health of our planet.

planet and our future.

Also remember to listen. Lots of people have ideas about alternative energy. What works for one person might not work for everyone. Everything costs money, and people need to decide the best ways to use it.

You are part of the next generation of energy consumers. You don't want the lights to go out on your plans for the future. Caring for Earth's resources is a big responsibility. Take small steps toward a bright energy future!

## A Green Investment

The United States has made
an investment in green energy.
Now more than ever, the government is creating new laws
and giving more money to
investigate alternative energy
options. Government agencies
are working to develop low-
carbon technologies and urging
carmakers to design more fuel-
efficient automobiles. They are
looking for ways to reduce
the use of fossil fuels in power
plants and working to expand
the power grid to get energy
to consumers from solar- and
wind-powered plants. Alternative
energy has become a national
priority, so get involved in the
discussion. We all need to play
a part as citizens of Earth.

# Glossary

**biofuels** — transportation fuels created from biomass

**biogas** — gas created by the decomposition of natural materials

**biomass** — natural products and waste that can be made into usable energy

**condenses** — turns from steam back to liquid water

**compost** — natural materials that can be used to create rich soil for new plants

**efficient** — operating in a way that creates the least waste of time, effort, or energy

**emissions** — substances released into the air

**enzymes** — substances that can create a chemical change in another substance

**evaporates** — turns from liquid water into a gas that enters the air

**fossil fuels** — fuels, including coal, oil, and natural gas, made from the remains of ancient organisms

**geysers** — holes in Earth's crust that let out hot water and steam

**phantom load** — electricity used by appliances when they are turned off

**photovoltaic cells** — small devices that absorb the sun's light and convert it to electricity

**sediment** — small bits of matter, such as rocks or sand, that settle to the bottom of a liquid

**thermal** — having to do with heat

**tidal barrage** — structure that dams the water from tides flowing toward and away from shore

**turbines** — machines that transform the energy of a moving object into mechanical power to generate electricity

# Investigate Further

## MORE BOOKS TO READ

Gleason, Carrie. *Geothermal Energy: Using Earth's Furnace*. New York: Crabtree Publishing Company, 2008.

Raum, Elizabeth. *Fueling the Future: Wind Energy*. Chicago: Heinemann Library, 2008.

Rooney, Anne. *Solar Power*. Pleasantville, N.Y.: Gareth Stevens Publishing, 2008.

Wines, Jacquie. *You Can Save the Planet: 50 Ways You Can Make a Difference*. New York: Scholastic, 2008.

## INTERNET SITES

FactHound offers a safe, fun way to find Internet sites related to this book. All of the sites on FactHound have been researched by our staff.

Here's all you do:
Visit *www.facthound.com*
FactHound will fetch the best sites for you!

# Index

# About the Author

Dana Meachen Rau is the author of more than 200 books for children, covering topics in science, history, geography, and hobbies. She stays warm by the solar heat coming through her office window, always uses both sides of the paper, and tries to make sure her recycling bin is fuller than her trash can. She lives with her family in Burlington, Connecticut.